The Royal Mummies:

Remains from Ancient Egypt

by Eric Kudalis

Consultant:

Dr. Salima Ikram

Department of Egyptology

American University in Cairo

CAPSTONE
HIGH-INTEREST
BOOKS

an imprint of Capstone Press
Mankato, Minnesota

Capstone High-Interest Books are published by Capstone Press
151 Good Counsel Drive, P.O. Box 669, Mankato, Minnesota 56002
http://www.capstone-press.com

Library of Congress Cataloging-in-Publication Data
Kudalis, Eric, 1960–
    The royal mummies: remains from ancient Egypt/by Eric Kudalis.
    p. cm.—(Mummies)
    Includes bibliographical references and index.
    Summary: Describes royal mummies of Ancient Egypt, some of the most famous royal mummies, how the Ancient Egyptians made mummies, how scientists study them, and what they can teach us about the past.
    ISBN 0-7368-1308-X (hardcover)
    1. Mummies—Egypt—Juvenile literature. [1. Mummies. 2. Kings, queens, rulers, etc.] I. Title. II. Series.
DT62.M7 K83 2003
383'.3'0932—dc21   2001007935

Editorial Credits
Carrie Braulick, editor; Karen Risch, product planning editor; Kia Adams, designer;
    Linda Clavel, illustrator; Jo Miller, photo researcher

Photo Credits
Barry Iverson/Woodfin Camp & Associates, Inc., 7, 10, 20
Bettmann/CORBIS, 23
Charles & Josette Lenars/CORBIS, 13
Gianni Dagli Orti/CORBIS, cover, 16
Nowitz/Folio, Inc., 15
Roger Wood/CORBIS, 4
Scala/Art Resource, NY, 24
Reuters/Timepix, 29
Underwood & Underwood/CORBIS, 26

1 2 3 4 5 6 07 06 05 04 03 02

Table of Contents

Features

Learn About:
- Locations of royal mummies
- Ancient Egyptian beliefs
- Pharaohs of ancient Egypt

Ahmed el-Rassul found Pinudjem II's tomb in Deir el-Bahari.

Chapter One

A Royal Discovery

In 1871, Ahmed el-Rassul was searching for his lost goat in a region of Egypt called Deir el-Bahari. This region is located along the western bank of the Nile River.

Ahmed found the goat at the bottom of a hill. He then discovered a doorway leading to a tomb. The ancient Egyptians carved tombs in cliffs near the Nile River thousands of years ago.

Ahmed told his brother Hussein about his discovery. Ahmed and Hussein found about 40 mummies in the tomb. These mummies were ancient Egyptian kings known as pharaohs and members of their families.

The tomb belonged to a pharaoh named Pinudjem II. This pharaoh died about 969 B.C. Among the other rulers in the tomb was Ramesses II. Ramesses II was one of ancient Egypt's best-known pharaohs. He ruled Egypt for 67 years between 1279 and 1212 B.C.

The brothers were more interested in the tomb's treasures than the mummies. The ancient Egyptians often placed gold statues, jars, and jewels with royal mummies. The brothers became wealthy selling artifacts from Pinudjem II's tomb during the next several years.

Attracting the Police

In the late 1880s, police noticed the brothers' activities. Robbing tombs was a crime. The police asked the brothers where they found the treasures. Ahmed and Hussein did not reveal their secret. But their brother Mohammed told police about the crime. Mohammed led the police to the tomb on July 6, 1881.

News of the discovery spread quickly. So many royal mummies had never been found in one place.

The ancient Egyptian empire became powerful during the reign of Ramesses II.

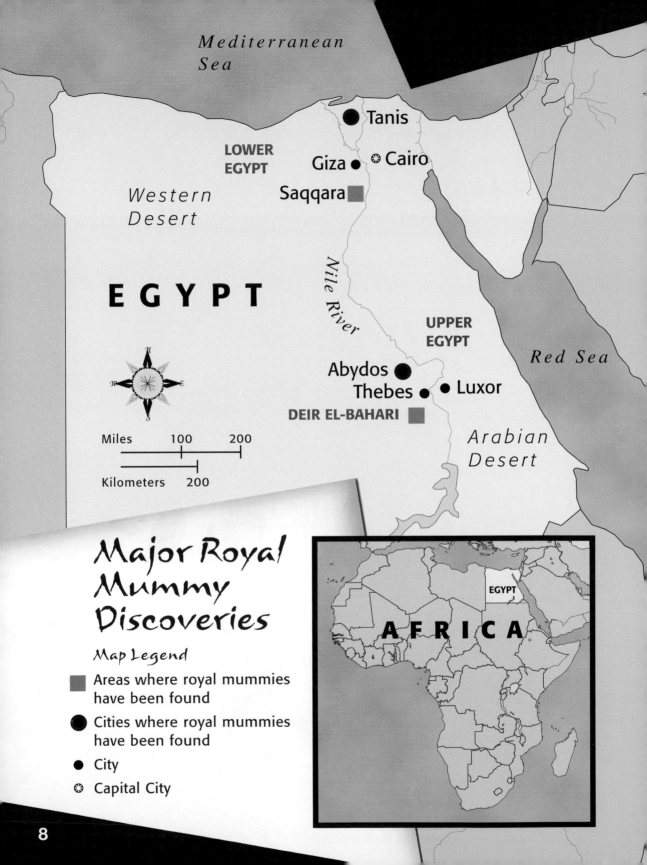

Mediterranean Sea

Tanis

LOWER EGYPT

Giza ● ⊛ Cairo

Saqqara ■

Western Desert

E G Y P T

Nile River

UPPER EGYPT

Abydos ●
Thebes ● ● Luxor

DEIR EL-BAHARI ■

Red Sea

Arabian Desert

Miles   100   200

Kilometers   200

Major Royal Mummy Discoveries

Map Legend

■ Areas where royal mummies have been found

● Cities where royal mummies have been found

● City

⊛ Capital City

EGYPT

A F R I C A

Mummies of Egypt

Ancient Egyptians believed they needed to be mummified to live in another world after death. They used chemicals to embalm bodies. The embalming process preserved the bodies.

Ancient Egyptians made both pharaohs and other important members of their society into mummies. Scientists believe that the ancient Egyptians made nearly 70 million mummies throughout about 3,000 years.

Royal Mummy Tombs

The ancient Egyptians placed royal mummies in large tombs called pyramids. The most famous tombs are the three pyramids near Giza. This city is located on the Nile's west bank in northern Egypt. Ancient Egyptians also built hidden underground tombs for the pharaohs.

The pharaohs prepared their tombs for the afterlife before they died. They stocked their tombs with golden statues, jewels, and other treasures.

Field of Reeds

The ancient Egyptians' afterlife was the Field of Reeds. To enter the afterlife, the soul needed to answer a series of questions. Ancient Egyptians wrote the answers on rolls of paper called papyrus and placed them in tombs. They followed this practice to make sure the questions were answered correctly.

Learn About:

Learn About:
- Mummy features
- The embalming process
- Burying royal mummies

The ancient Egyptian embalming process preserved the facial tissues of pharaoh Tuthmosis III.

Chapter Two

How Ancient Egyptians Made Mummies

All living things decay after death. Small organisms called bacteria and fungi eat a dead body's tissues. The tissues then break down until only the bones remain.

The ancient Egyptian embalming process prevented the growth of bacteria and fungi. The dead bodies became mummies instead of decaying. Mummies may have skin, eyes, and other preserved body parts.

Making Mummies

The ancient Egyptians developed ways to make mummies over thousands of years. Around 5000 B.C., they buried dead bodies in the desert sand. The hot, dry conditions quickly dried out the bodies. Bacteria and fungi cannot grow without moisture. The bodies also were protected from weather conditions such as strong winds. The dry conditions and shelter turned the bodies into natural mummies.

Eventually, ancient Egyptians looked for better ways to make mummies. They wanted to bury rulers in expensive coffins and place them in tombs. But the bodies decayed when they were not buried in the sand.

Around 2600 B.C., the ancient Egyptians started to remove the internal organs so the bodies would dry better. They then wrapped the bodies in cloth. But these bodies still decayed.

The ancient Egyptians wrapped bodies
to help keep them dry.

13

Removing the Brain

By about 2000 B.C., the ancient Egyptians had developed a very successful way to make mummies. They followed several steps to embalm bodies. They first brought a body to embalmers. These skilled workers washed the body in water from the Nile River. The embalmers stretched the body on a wooden table. They inserted a metal rod through the nose to break through to the brain.

Embalmers then used a long hook to dig out the brain. They poured melted resin through the nose. This sticky, dark substance comes from the sap of some trees. It prevented bacteria from growing inside the skull. Embalmers then threw out the brain. The ancient Egyptians believed the brain had no purpose.

Removing Organs

Embalmers made a slit in the body's side to remove the internal organs. They removed the lungs, stomach, intestines, and liver. They left the heart in the body because they believed it was needed for the afterlife.

Embalmers cleaned the organs with wine and dried them with a type of salt called natron. They covered the organs with resin. Embalmers then wrapped them in linen. They often stored the organs in containers called canopic jars. They placed the body on a slanted embalming table to allow the body's liquids to drip out.

The ancient Egyptians stored internal organs in canopic jars.

Cleaning and Wrapping

Embalmers washed the inside of the body with
wine and dried it with linen cloths. Embalmers
then stuffed and covered the body with natron.
The natron caused the body to dry out in about
40 days.

The embalmers then stuffed the body with linen, sawdust, herbs, soil, and more natron. These materials kept the body dry and helped the body keep its shape. Embalmers placed jewels on the body, applied makeup, and styled the hair.

Next, embalmers poured oils and resin over the body. Embalmers then wrapped the body in layers of linen strips. They used resin between each layer of wrappings to make them stick. Embalmers often placed jewels and small treasures between the linen layers. They sometimes placed a gold mask over the person's head.

Burial

The wrapped body was then ready for burial. Ancient Egyptians placed the mummy in a coffin. This coffin usually was nested inside several other coffins. The outer coffins usually were wooden. For pharaohs, the inner coffin often was made of gold. The ancient Egyptians then carried the coffins to the tomb.

At the tomb, they placed the coffins into a sarcophagus. This stone coffin protected the other coffins.

Making an Ancient Egyptian Mummy

Step 1

Removing, Cleaning, and Storing Organs

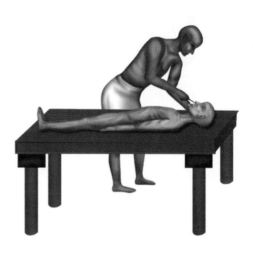

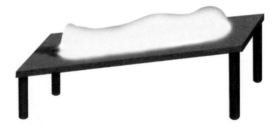

Step 2

Drying the Body

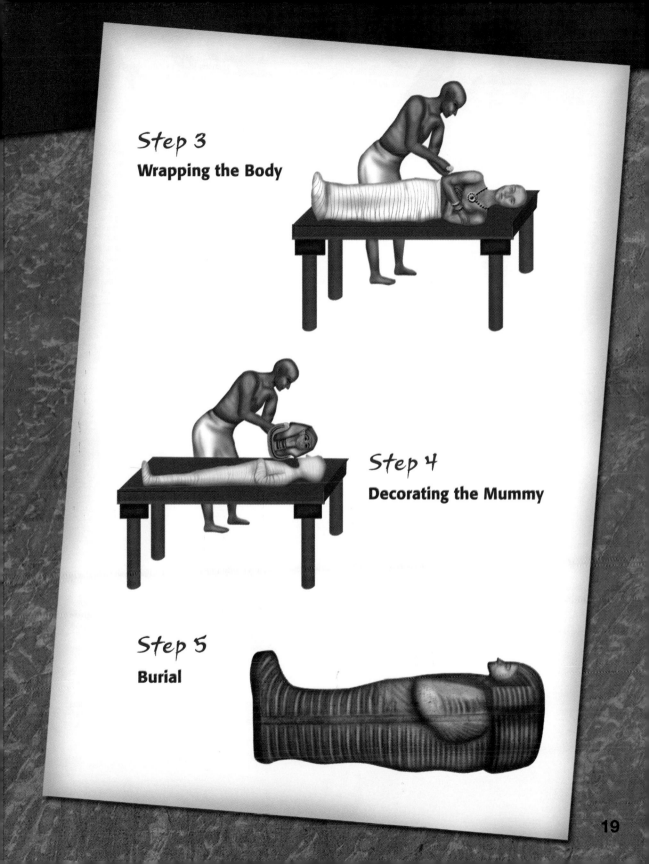

Step 3
Wrapping the Body

Step 4
Decorating the Mummy

Step 5
Burial

Learn About:
- Scientific methods
- X-rays and CT scans
- Ancient Egyptians' health

Scientists studied x-rays to estimate that Tuthmosis II died when he was about 30.

Chapter Three

Royal Mummy Secrets Revealed

Scientists study mummies to learn how the ancient Egyptians lived. The scientists can learn about diseases that affected them. They may be able to find out how some people who were made into mummies died.

X-rays and CT Scans

Scientists use x-rays and CT scans to study mummies. X-ray machines take pictures of the inside of a body. CT scanners are similar to x-ray machines. But CT scans allow scientists to see internal body parts from different angles at the same time. The view is displayed on a computer screen.

Through x-rays and CT scans, scientists have discovered that many ancient Egyptians had arthritis. This painful condition causes the bone joints to swell.

X-rays also showed that ancient Egyptians suffered from worn teeth. Wind caused the desert sand to blow around. The sand mixed with the ancient Egyptians' bread dough. The hard bread wore down their teeth. The teeth eventually became stumps.

Tissue Samples

Scientists also take tissue samples from mummies. They use a long metal needle to scrape away a small part of a mummy's tissue. They can look at the tissue more closely under a microscope or mix it with chemicals to find out what diseases affected the person. Scientists may take tissue from the stomach or intestines to learn about the person's diet.

Through tissue samples, scientists have discovered that some ancient Egyptians had parasites. These small organisms live on or inside people or other animals. Some ancient Egyptians had parasites called tapeworms. These worms usually live in the intestines.

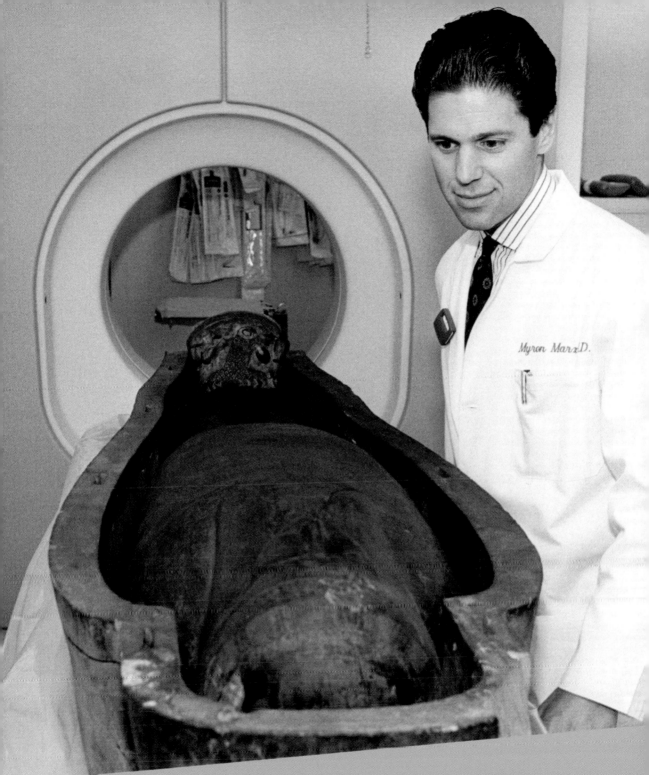

Scientists can place mummies in CT scanners to view their internal body parts.

Scientific examinations showed that Ramesses II suffered from arthritis.

Ramesses II Examined

Ramesses II was one of ancient Egypt's most famous pharaohs. He was more than 90 years old when he died in 1212 B.C. Most Egyptians at this time lived only about 30 years. During his reign, the Egyptian empire grew powerful and wealthy. Ramesses II built many temples and monuments throughout the empire.

Examinations showed that Ramesses II had serious medical problems. He probably was in great pain by the time he died. Ramesses II suffered from severe arthritis. He had hardened arteries. These tubes carry blood from the heart to other parts of the body. Hardened arteries can block the flow of blood.

Ramesses II had gum disease, and his teeth were badly worn. Gum disease occurs when the gums become infected. The ancient Egyptians did not have supplies to take good care of their teeth.

No Records

Ancient Egyptians never recorded their embalming methods. Artwork on some ancient Egyptian tombs and coffins show people embalming. But they provide no directions for how to embalm.

A Greek historian named Herodotus wrote about the embalming process when he traveled to Egypt about 2,500 years ago. He published his findings in a book called *Histories*. Another Greek historian named Diodorus Siculus wrote about the ancient Egyptian embalming process about 400 years later.

Howard Carter (second from left) helped carry artifacts out of Tutankhamun's tomb.

Chapter Four

Mummy Myths

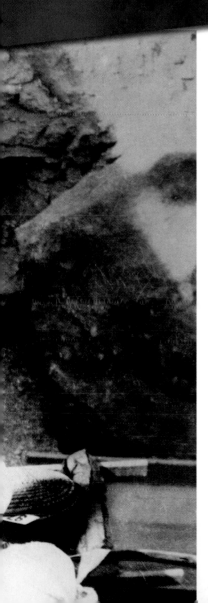

People have told stories about mummies for thousands of years. Mummies were evil characters in many of these stories. The stories have caused some people to fear mummies.

Tutankhamun's Curse

In 1922, Lord Carnavon and archaeologist Howard Carter discovered Tutankhamun's tomb. Tutankhamun became a pharaoh at age 9. He died around 1300 B.C. when he was about 18 years old.

Tutankhamun's tomb was well preserved. Grave robbers had not destroyed it. The tomb contained many artifacts made of gold. These items included a mask, slippers, furniture, and game boards.

Lord Carnavon grew sick after a mosquito bite became infected. He died on April 5, 1923. Many people believed that Carnavon died because Tutankhamun's tomb had a curse. They thought his death was Tutankhamun's revenge for disturbing his tomb.

Using Mummies

During the 1600s, many Europeans ground thousands of mummies into powder. They believed the powder cured illnesses.

More Stories

Another mummy story says Ramesses II lifted one of his arms and pointed at the people who moved him. The workers believed the mummy was threatening them. After studying the event, some scientists believe the arm rose because the mummy had been lying in the sun. The sun warmed the body and caused its muscles to shrink.

Scientists do not believe royal mummies are evil or that they carry curses. But mummies will continue to fascinate people. Scientists hope to find more royal mummies in the future. They hope their efforts will reveal new information about ancient Egyptian culture.

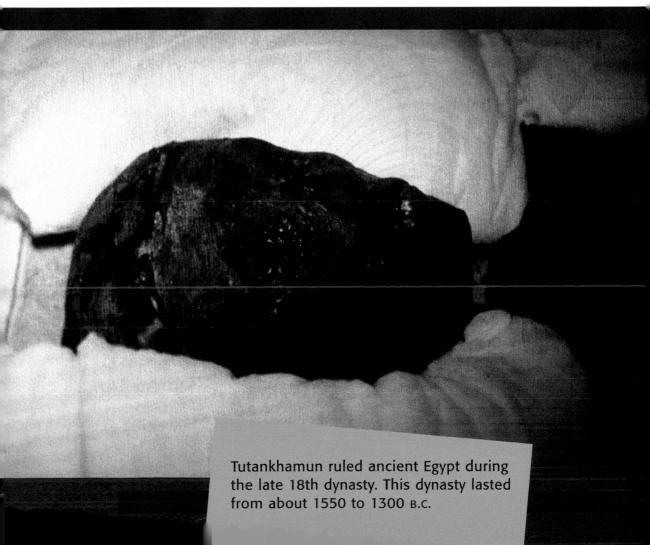

Tutankhamun ruled ancient Egypt during the late 18th dynasty. This dynasty lasted from about 1550 to 1300 B.C.

Words to Know

arthritis (ar-THRYE-tiss)—a disease that makes people's bone joints swollen and painful

artifact (ART-uh-fakt)—an object used in the past that was made by people

bacteria (bak-TIHR-ee-uh)—very small living organisms; bacteria eat the soft tissue of dead bodies.

fungi (FUHN-jye)—a type of organism that has no leaves, flowers, or roots

natron (NAY-tron)—a type of salt

parasite (PA-ruh-site)—a small organism that lives on or inside a person or animal

pharaoh (FAIR-oh)—a king of ancient Egypt

resin (REZ-in)—a sticky substance that comes from the sap of some trees

sarcophagus (sar-KAH-fuh-guhs)—a stone coffin; the ancient Egyptians placed inner coffins into a sarcophagus.

x-ray machine (EKS-ray muh-SHEEN)—a machine that takes pictures of the inside of a body

To Learn More

Mason, Paul. *Mummies.* Mysteries of the Past.
    Austin, Texas: Raintree Steck-Vaughn, 2002.

Tanaka, Shelley. *Secrets of the Mummies:*
    Uncovering the Bodies of Ancient Egyptians.
    New York: Hyperion/Madison Press, 1999.

Wilcox, Charlotte. *Mummies, Bones, and Body*
    Parts. Minneapolis: Carolrhoda Books, 2000.

Places of Interest

The Egyptian Museum
Tahrir Square
Cairo, Egypt

National Museum of Natural History
Smithsonian Institution
10th Street and Constitution Avenue NW
Washington, DC 20560

University of Chicago Museum
Oriental Institute
1155 East 58th Street
Chicago, IL 60637

Internet Sites

Egyptian Mummies
http://www.si.edu/resource/faq/nmnh/mummies.htm

Neferchichi's Tomb—Kids Page
http://www.neferchichi.com/kids.html

Unwrapped—The Mysterious World of Mummies
http://tlc.discovery.com/tlcpages/mummies/
  mummies.html

Index

10/02